NDS?

Unexpected Animal Friendships from around the World

by Erica Sirotich

HARPER
An Imprint of HarperCollinsPublishers

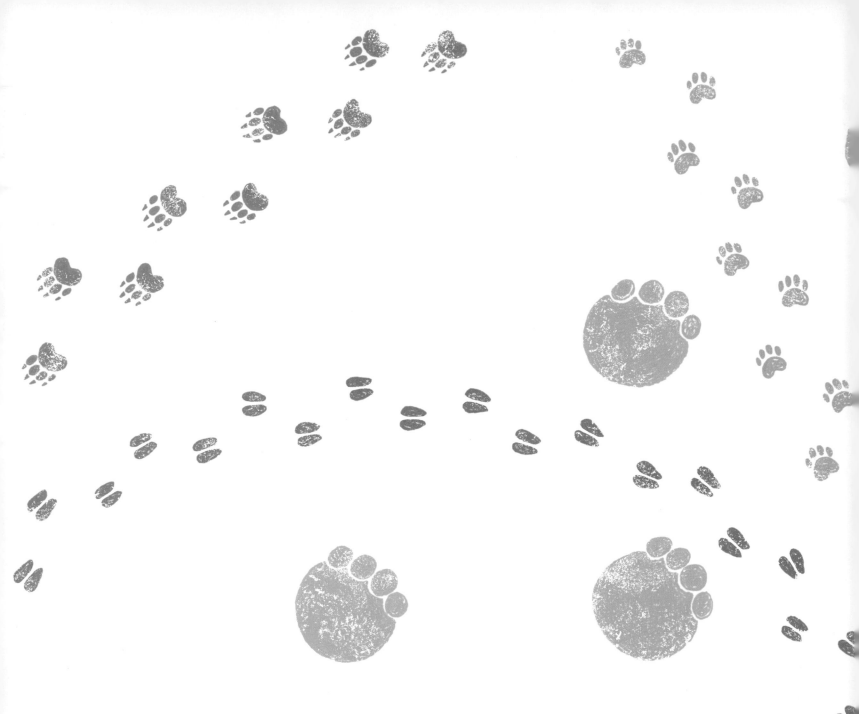

Can We Be Friends?: Unexpected Animal Friendships from around the World • Copyright © 2020 by Erica Sirotich • All rights reserved. Manufactured in China. • No part of this book may be used or reproduced in any manner whatsoever without written permission except in the case of brief quotations embodied in critical articles and reviews. For information address HarperCollins Children's Books, a division of HarperCollins Publishers, 195 Broadway, New York, NY 10007. • www.harpercollinschildrens.com Library of Congress Control Number: 2019944982 • ISBN 978-0-06-294158-9 • The artist used brushes, ink, and digital color to create the illustrations for this book. Typography by Honee Jang • 20 21 22 23 24 SCP 10 9 8 7 6 5 4 3 2 1 ❖ First Edition

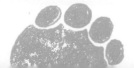

For my friends
Rob, Candy, Julie, and Candice

Can you be friends
with somebody who
is very different
and not at all like you?

Let's see.

My shell is my house.
I'm a hundred or more!
I like the calm, quiet hush
of the forest floor.

I'm big all around,
but I'm still a calf.
I make a loud, rowdy ruckus
when I take a bath.

After a tidal wave hit Kenya, Africa, baby hippo Owen couldn't find his family. But soon he was rescued and moved to a nearby forest sanctuary. There, a very old giant tortoise named Mzee became his friend. The two foraged and ate together, waded in the water together, and napped in the sun together. Like a true friend, Mzee helped Owen grow into a big, strong, happy hippopotamus. In fact, within a few years, Owen grew to be much larger than his tortoise companion!

My coat is spotted,
and I need to run.
I'm shy; I shiver
when I meet someone.

My fur is golden,
and I love to chew.
I wag, wiggle, BARK
when I see someone new.

At a zoo in Virginia, Kumbali the cheetah cub was the runt of the litter. Zookeepers had to bottle-feed the baby and teach him how to be a big cat. Kumbali felt unsure and longed for a friend. At a nearby animal shelter, puppy Kago was feeling the same way. So the zookeepers decided to bring the cub and the puppy together. When Kago arrived, he was so playful, and just like a cheetah, he loved to run! Kumbali and Kago became fast friends and live together at the zoo to this day.

My trunk collects water
to squirt and spray.
My feet STOMP, STOMP
when I run and play.

My fleece is fluffy.
I'm woolly and white.
I baa, baa, BOUNCE
on my hooves, so light.

Can we be friends?

Of course!

At a South Africa sanctuary,

an elephant calf named Themba wanted a friend. But there were no other elephants around. One day, his caretakers introduced Albert the sheep, and after a rocky first visit, they became best buddies. They did everything together except take baths—elephants love water, but sheep do not like to get wet!

It's almost bedtime,
so I build a nest.
I sign, "*Sleep* now, Koko,"
settle down, and rest.

It's dark outside now.
We find a warm spot.
We snore, snuggle, *purrrrrr*,
wake up, spar, and swat.

Can we be friends?

Certainly!

Koko the gorilla was born in a California zoo. Her caretaker, Penny, knew gorillas were very smart. Penny brought Koko to live with her at a research center called the Gorilla Foundation. She taught Koko sign language so she could understand her better. Using her signs, Koko asked Penny for a kitten! Over the years, Koko adopted several kitten friends, including All Ball, Smoky, Ms. Gray, Lips, and Ms. Black (she named them herself). At bedtime, Koko built herself a comfy nest out of blankets, towels, and other soft things. Kittens can sleep anywhere, but Koko's kittens loved to join her for a nap in her nest.

I walk on the land.
I dig, and I chase.
My paws pitter-patter
from place to place.

I swim in the sea.
I soar, and I sail.
I swoosh, splish, SPLASH
with the turn of my tail.

In Ireland, a dog named Ben jumps into the ocean every day to swim and play with Duggie, a wild bottlenose dolphin. If Ben swims too long or too far and gets tired, Duggie gives him a ride back to shore. What a great friend!

Whose friend will **YOU** be?

Glossary

adopt: To take someone in and become their parent or caregiver.

animal shelter: A place where dogs, cats, and other pets can live while waiting to be adopted into new families.

calf: The name for certain types of baby animals, such as cows, whales, elephants, and hippopotamuses.

caretaker: Someone who looks after other people or animals.

forage: To search for food.

forest floor: The ground level of a forest, where plants and trees grow and many animals live.

rescue: To help or save an animal or person who is lost or in trouble.

runt: The smallest baby in a litter of baby animals. Sometimes the runt needs extra help and care to grow up to be big and strong.

sanctuary: A place where animals that have been rescued can live in a setting that is similar to their natural habitat.

sign language: A language that uses hand and body gestures to communicate words and ideas.

zoo: A place where different types of animals are kept, where people can visit and learn about them.

Sources

- Cocks, Hayley, dir. *Wild & Woolly: An Elephant and His Sheep*. Doha, Qatar: Rock Wallaby Productions, 2011.
- Edwards, Roberta. *Best Friends: The True Story of Owen and Mzee*. New York: Penguin Young Readers, 2007.
- Hatkoff, Isabella, Craig Hatkoff, and Paula Kahumbu. *Owen & Mzee: The True Story of a Remarkable Friendship*. New York: Scholastic, 2006.
- Holland, Jennifer S. *Unlikely Friendships: 47 Remarkable Stories from the Animal Kingdom*. New York: Workman, 2011.
- Metro Richmond Zoo. "Kumbali and Kago, Cheetah Cub and Puppy Friendship." Posted October 6, 2015. http://metrorichmondzoo.com/kumbali/.
- Patterson, Francine. *Koko's Kitten*. New York: Scholastic, 2010.
- *Unlikely Animal Friends*. Season 1, episode 3, "Dogs Gone Wild." Aired November 12, 2012, on National Geographic.
- Vessels, Jane. "Koko's Kitten." *National Geographic*, January 1985.

Read More About It!

- Visit ericasirotich.com for more resources and videos about unexpected animal friends from around the world.
- Read Animal Fact Guide's articles on unlikely animal friends: https://animalfactguide.com/tag/unlikely-animal-friends/.
- Watch videos of unlikely animal friends from National Geographic: https://video.nationalgeographic.com/video/unlikely-animal-friends.
- Watch videos of animal odd couples from *Nature* on PBS: http://www.pbs.org/wnet/nature/animal-odd-couples-introduction/7958/.
- Learn about the amazing life and abilities of Koko the Gorilla at the Gorilla Foundation's website: https://www.koko.org/
- Learn facts about all kinds of animals and explore activities at the San Diego Zoo's great kids' website: https://kids.sandiegozoo.org/.
- Explore New York elementary school students' projects about animal friendships: sites.google.com/williamsvillek12.org/mapleeastlibrary/projects/animal-friendships